KEYS TO THE SPIRIT WORLD

AN EASY TO USE HANDBOOK FOR CONTACTING YOUR SPIRIT GUIDES

JENNIFER O'NEILL

empowered
Empath

Keys to the Spirit World, LLC

Kailua, HI 96734

www.keystothespiritworld.com

Formatting: Keys to the Spirit World LLC

This is a work of fiction. Names, characters, places, and incidents either are
the product of the author's imagination or are used fictitiously, and any
resemblance to locales, events, business establishments, or actual persons—
living or dead—is entirely coincidental.

CHAPTER 1

WHAT IS A SPIRIT GUIDE?

*M*any people have heard of Spirit Guides, however, a lot of people are left wondering, "What exactly is a Spirit Guide?" This is a really great question and I am happy to answer it. But in order to answer this question, I would like to start out by giving you a little bit more information, or knowledge, on your creation as a spiritual being.

When all spirits were created, you (as a spirit) were created with the ability to incarnate here on earth. In other words, you have the unique ability to exist not only in the spiritual realm, in your natural state of existence, but in the physical realm as well. Amazing! So you were created with the ability to live as many lifetimes as you wish here in the physical realm, in order to learn and grow spiritually to the best of your ability. You choose when to incarnate here on earth, as well as how many lifetimes you would like to experience. This allows you to gain knowledge that is only possible for you to obtain by living many lifetimes in the physical realm, by being a human being, not just a spiritual being.

With this wonderful ability certain precautions, or safe-guards, were put into place to make sure that you get the most possible spiritual growth out of each reincarnation. What is reincarnation? The same as incarnation; choosing to be born into the physical world in order to learn and grow spiritually from the encounters you have here on earth, throughout each lifetime. One of the safeguards put into place for your trip into the physical realm was to make sure that you never make this transition alone, or without any spiritual guidance from the "Other Side." Why? Well, because it makes good sense. Just think about it; you are a spiritual being having a physical experience, not the other way around. When you adapt into the physical realm, there are a lot of adjustments that need to be made. During this transi-tion you can also get what I call "spiritual amnesia." What is spiritual amnesia? It's when you forget about the spiritual realm, and your natural state of existence. Why should it matter if you forget about the spiritual realm, why you are here on earth, while in the physical realm? Because, if this happens, you also forget about the many spiritual tools that you have access to. These tools, in actuality, work very well in the physical realm. However, it is hard to access some-thing that you have forgotten about. There are many things that you are capable of, things that are not taught to you when you are in physical form. In fact, you when you are in physical form, most people are taught how *not* to use their spiritual tools. It is for these reasons mentioned, that you are required to have some form of spiritual guidance.

Spiritual guidance comes to you through different avenues, and in different forms. One important avenue is by the way of a Spirit Guide. Spirit Guides are regular spirits, just like you, who have incarnated here on earth at least one time before. These spirits make a choice, or choose, to become a Spirit Guide to other spirits. It is something that they wish to do, like a career path. When a spirit chooses Spirit Guide as a path they wish to pursue, they are required to go through a training process in which they are specially taught to do the job. The preparation is thorough and intense (since their job requires dealing with the hard headedness we have become so accustomed to when we get here).

So when you choose to reincarnate on earth, one of the things that is essential before you make the trip, is to choose a trained Spirit Guide. This Spirit Guide will then help you to get things in order for your up and coming journey. They will help you most importantly to create your life path or your chart. Your life path or chart is a spiritual blueprint of your physical life, mapping out your journey. How does this happen? You and your Spirit Guide will map out your chart together, by giving serious thought to all of the things that you would like to experience and accomplish while you are here on earth, in the physical realm. This allows your Spirit Guide to have a very clear vision of what you are trying to accomplish from your own perspective. They have, in fact, helped you to create the very path that you are on now!

When you incarnate, and you are no longer on the "Other Side" (you are now on the physical plane), your Spirit Guide's job is to look after you. They help to guide you according to the plan, or life path, that you designed for yourself, together on the "Other Side." They try their best to keep you "on track" so to speak. They help to give you courage, strength, and knowledge, all the while watching out for your charts. However, they have other jobs too. Those jobs also include recruiting other specialized guides or Angels if needed, as well as helping you with spiritual or energetic protection. All with the same purpose, to help you achieve the things that you are here to achieve, in accordance with your chart. If you get way off track, which is common, your Spirit Guide will do whatever they can to steer you back in the right direction.

Spirit Guides cannot be anyone that you know from this lifetime. Because that would mean at some point, while you were here on earth, you were without any spiritual guidance, and that simply cannot happen. In other words, just to make it clear, your Spirit Guide is not your grandmother, dad, sister, or friend from this lifetime. You cannot have been alive at the same time, during this lifetime, as your current Spirit Guide. They can be, however, someone that you were close to in another lifetime, like a friend or relative from a past life or different lifetime. In fact, that is very common!

Although you have one main Spirit Guide, you can have other Spirit Guides join you throughout your lifetime journey. The one that I have been talking about up until this point is your main Spirit Guide, or your general Spirit Guide. The Spirit Guide who stays with you always, from birth, until you leave this physical plane. However, you can also have other specialized Spirit Guides that come into your life and stay with you for a shorter period of time. They can be with you for a long or a short duration depending on what is necessary or happening in your life at the time. These specialized Spirit Guides come in at different times of your life in order to help teach you about something that you are trying to learn, or help you with a skill that you are trying to develop. Things such as Reiki, healing, cooking, sports, health, etcetera, may require a different type of Spiritual Guide. They can also come in during periods of hardship, like if you are battling an addiction or having a health issue. During this time, your general Spirit Guide is still working in your corner, on your behalf, as your main Spirit Guide. When other specialized Spirit Guides are called in, they all work together as a team. One does not bow out so that another one can take its place. In fact, like I mentioned before, your general Spirit Guide is usually the one who recruits other specialized guides in the first place, in order to help you and give you further guidance. There is no competition among Spirit Guides, they all have the utmost respect for each other, and have your best interest at heart. They come from a place of guidance and love.

Besides recruiting specialized Spirit Guides to help you in time of need, your general Spirit Guide's job is to also, as I mentioned before, work with your Angels. There are many different types of Angels on the "Other Side" (which is a whole different book), so when your Spirit Guide sees that you are in need (if you have not asked for them already), they will recruit or call in Angels. They know which Angels to call upon and how many to bring in. Just like Spirit Guides, Angels have different jobs, according to their phylum, so it is helpful that your Spirit Guide knows which ones to call upon. Your guide can also go to the higher phylum of Angels in order to request help to intervene with your chart if necessary. Spirit Guides do not have the authority to intervene with your charts, but Angels do. This might happen if you have strayed so far off your path that your chart may actually need to be altered. Getting off of your path this far usually happens because we exercise free will and stubbornness. Many times when people get frustrated and think that they have no spiritual guidance, it's not because they do not have any, it's because they have the right to ignore their Spirit Guides. Free will is very powerful! You have the right and ability to go against your own spiritual wishes or desires, which many people do a really good job of doing. Especially when they think what they really want differs on the physical plain from what they had originally intended when they were in the spiritual realm. When you get too far away, or disconnected, from who you are on a soul level, you can be enticed in other directions causing you to head down a dangerous or destructive road. That would be an instance when your Spirit Guide may have to take measures into their own hands and have your chart altered.

Your Spirit Guides are your protectors. As a spiritual being yourself, it is important that you have spiritual support, even if you choose to ignore it. However, if you are reading this book, most likely you have not chosen to ignore your Spirit Guides at all. Up until this point, you have probably just not had all of the knowledge required to advance your spirit communication skills and allow you to truly understand the entire process. In order to be successful, it is important that we cover all bases, which we will do here in this book.

CHAPTER 2

WHAT DO SPIRIT GUIDES LOOK LIKE?

*S*pirit Guides look just like regular people, like you and me. They come in all shapes and sizes, different heights and different races. Their eye color, age, and hair color varies, and they can be male or female. What does usually differ, however, is the way that they dress, or the way that they present themselves to you visually. You can see your Spirit Guides during dreams, meditation, or past life regression. When you see your Spirit Guide, they tend to dress in the time period of which they are most fond, or in a way that they think might trigger your memory of them.

Although many of you may not remember seeing your Spirit Guide, I am most certain you have probably felt them at one time or another. When you feel them, you will usually feel them behind you, like someone is standing there and when you turn around there is no one there. I have never run across anyone that has not had that feeling at some point in time. Most likely you have had it when you were alone. Have you ever had that feeling? Most people just brush it off when they realize that no one is there, or they get freaked out and walk around backwards for a little while, or sit with their back against the wall. It is also common for you to feel them behind you when you are driving in your car, usually over one of your shoulders. Then you look in the rearview mirror to make sure that no one is back there.

Why are you more likely to feel your Spirit Guide when you are alone? Because when you are alone you become very tuned in, and sensitive, to all of the energy around you. There is usually nothing else going on to divert your attention. When people are around you, it is much more distracting. They are making noise, and you concentrate on them and what they are doing, or you are engaging in conversation. If that isn't enough, to make things more awkward, your Spirit Guides can really be felt at night. If you are like my friend Dawn, you are probably thinking, "That's just great! I can never be alone now, especially at night! Or I am going to have to walk around with a bat in my hand, and sleep with one eye open!" Just remember Spirit Guides come with love and they are here for protection and guidance. The reason you can feel them more at night is because of the thickness of the veil. The veil is what separates the spirit realm from the physical realm and it is thinner at night; therefore, you are more sensitive to feeling spirit energy at night.

Children are usually very in tune with their Spirit Guides and they feel their presence often. They do not think much of it until they get older, then as young adults, because of their newly formed belief system, it begins to freak them out. So it is then that they will begin to tune it out as much as possible. It is a process most of us go through, unfortunately.

Often when my son was very young, he would see his Spirit Guide around wherever he was at the time. He would mention seeing Frank every now and again when he was around the house. Most nights he would tune in, or become very aware of the presence of his guide. Much of the time his

Spirit Guide would be walking on the front porch of our home, or he would show up at the end of his bed, while he was sleeping. He would notice him if he woke up in the middle of the night. Now in most instances, this would startle the majority of kids. They would run tell their parents, everyone would think the house was haunted and they would all want to move! Luckily for him, I was well aware of what he was seeing, and spirits were nothing to be afraid of in our household. They were a part of our life, so it was "normal" to feel them or see them. Needless to say, those experiences were not nearly as scary as they could have been, had the environment been a different one. What I mean by that is, if we had taken on the perspective or belief of spirits being scary.

My son could see his Spirit Guide clearly and he would describe him in great detail. His guide was about six feet tall with dark hair and dark eyes (probably brown, not black or anything). He dressed in a black suit, with a white undershirt, an overcoat, and a fedora hat. The era of dress was consistent with his Spirit Guide's last lifetime here on earth. We know this because when my son was older, I did a past life regression on him (my kids used to love to do this for fun), and he had a very clear memory of being with his Spirit Guide during one of his last lifetimes, sometime in the very early 1900s. He could see that they worked together in that lifetime and he knew roughly where they lived. He knew that his friend saved his life and that they were very good friends throughout that existence.

Dressing in the era of their last existence together may have been an attempt to try and present himself in a manner that my son would recognize him, or potentially trigger some internal memory, as not to frighten him. Or maybe he just liked the suit.

One day I asked my son if he knew why his Spirit Guide

was always walking on the front porch, and he said, "Yes, for protection and to watch over me!" A few nights after that conversation, his Spirit Guide began talking to me. At first it sounded a little far away, but then the voice became louder. It sounded like I was listening to an old radio that was mostly tuned in, but still a little fuzzy or static. He told me he was my son's Spirit Guide. I knew that he came to me because I had asked my son questions about him. That's what spirits do, they come in when you think about them; you may not be aware of this, but it is true. So, I asked him what his name was. In a chipper voice he responded, "Frank." Then he waited. I was surprised at the personality that came through in his voice, it was strong yet happy. I guess I expected his voice to be more serious or down to business sounding, but it wasn't. So I asked him why he was here.

He answered with a slight chuckle, "I am here for protection." Kind of like, you already know this, but I will be happy to confirm it for you! It was interesting that he told me exactly what my son already knew; kids are very good at receiving communication from their Spirit Guides. We had a few more words, and then Frank faded out. Which brings us to the next chapter...

CHAPTER 3

HOW DO SPIRIT GUIDES COMMUNICATE?

*S*o this brings us to the next chapter and something I find very interesting but people don't ask about very often: how do Spirit Guides communicate? I think this question is not asked very much because most people assume that they know the answer already. The interesting thing is, most of the time their assumptions are wrong. When I teach this subject in a class or a lecture, the students often realize that they are actually quite confused on how this spirit communication thing happens. People are often under the impression that Spirit Guides communicate with you through just one avenue, and when and if it happens you'll know it. I think the only reason for this assumption is that most of the time you just haven't given it too much thought. Because for some of you, the idea of thinking that you actually have some sort of control over how you communicate with your Spirit Guide probably seems a little far-fetched. Truthfully, some of you might even be on the fence about whether or not to believe in this whole Spirit Guide thing in the first place. But think about it, you really need to know more about how the communication process works in order to rule out any of those things anyway!

Spirit Guides communicate with you in various ways. Some are more common than others, and some of these avenues can have a very subtle approach to them, especially at first. In other words, it is important for you to be aware of the communication process in order to receive the information. Otherwise, you may just think that you are having random thoughts and disregard them when you are actually receiving information from your Spirit Guide.

Here are the most common ways Spirit Guides communicate with you, in no particular order:

#1 Through Telepathy

The first avenue I would like to address, and one of the most common ways for a Spirit Guide to communicate with you, is through telepathy. Telepathy is when you receive information by hearing or seeing something in your mind, or what is called "your mind's eye" that another person (or in this case a spirit) has intentionally put there as an attempt to communicate with you. In other words, they are trying to relay a message to you. It can be in the form of words, letters, pictures, or a combination of all of these things. Telepathy is something Spirit Guides will utilize in order to communicate short bursts of information to you. For instance, if your Spirit Guide thinks it would be useful for you to buy a certain book. Maybe that book contains information that would be useful to you. Out of nowhere that book might pop into your head, an image of the book, or the title to the book. Or maybe you are trying to think of a great place to take a vacation, and out of nowhere a destination you never even thought of pops into your head. These are just examples; just remember it is used for short bursts of information, as well as yes or no kind of information.

#2 Blocks of Thought

Another popular way of receiving spirit communication is by receiving blocks of thought. This happens when the information being relayed to you is too much information to give you in just a few pictures or words. Imagine it like this: when you download information from the Internet onto your computer, you get a bunch of information compiled together giving you an overall picture real quick. This avenue is usually utilized with people who are more advanced and know where it is coming from. Also, anyone who is really tapped into his or her creative side will utilize this avenue often. Artists, musicians, and writers use this process a lot. They will receive whole concepts this way, then they can fill in all of the little details themselves. Things like an idea for a song, or a vision of a character, or a plot for a book or movie. They will receive the overall vision and then they can elaborate upon it. As a psychic, this is an avenue that my Spirit Guides often utilize. When I meet someone, I get huge blocks of information on that particular person. Things like what type of person they are, things they are struggling with now or in the past, what their intentions are, etcetera.

#3 A "Knowing"

This is a bit different, and in my experience, not everyone utilizes this gift. It is tied into a psychic ability people can have called claircognizance. Claircognizance is sometimes used in conjunction with other avenues of communication as a way of "confirming" the information you are receiving in from your Spirit Guide. This "knowing" is a feeling you will get across your entire being, on a soul level. It is when you already know something is true as if it has already happened. You feel it in the body and it is something you know as fact. You will know immediately if you utilize this form of communication, because it is hard to explain to people who have not experienced it. If this does not sound familiar to you, this is most likely an avenue which you will not use.

#4 Dreams and Meditation

Communication through dreams and meditation is also quite common, when you remember them. Many times people have a hard time remembering what information they receive during the night. When you fall asleep you naturally align yourself spiritually; in fact, this is why you need to sleep. It's not just to rest your body. It has been scientifically proven that your body gets enough rest during times of sitting throughout the day that it does not require a long period of sleep to recover. Sleep, however, has been programmed into your Soul DNA to make sure that you have a consistent time each day in which you allow yourself to spiritually align again. Why? Because even if you were very aware of the requirements of your spiritual being needing to be in spiritual alignment at least once everyday, what are the chances that everyone would do it and do it consistently? About zero! That being said, you do it anyway and it's called sleep. During this time, your belief system comes down, and you naturally reach higher consciousness. When you reach higher consciousness, you are able to shift dimensions with ease and maneuver the spirit world effortlessly. You can see loved ones who have passed over. This is why many times when you awaken from a dream where you have seen or visited with a loved one who has passed, you can't explain why but it feels very different, very real. Then you wake up, your belief system is promptly restored to the physical realm, and you call it a dream.

My daughter used to see loved ones all of the time during the night and they would have long conversations with her. She would wake up and tell me about her "visits." See, in our household they are visits, because we are all very well aware of the dimensional shifting that takes place, but to other people they are mistaken for dreams. So during this dream state you can get quite a lot of information from your spirit guide. As far as meditation is concerned, when done properly, your belief system is also left behind and you begin to touch lightly upon dimensional shifting. When this takes place, the spirit communication will become part of the process if you wish.

#5 Hearing With the "Inner Ear"

You may or may not have heard this term before: "inner ear." This is a term you will become very familiar with if you are learning to develop your intuition or spirit communication. What this means is that you hear things in your head from the "inner ear" so it sounds like it is coming from within your inner being, instead of outside of your being like when you hear with the outer ear. For instance, you know how you can recall a conversation that you had or a song that you heard recently and you can hear it just by remembering it? That is what it is like to hear something with your "inner ear," only it is not something that you are reaching for or you are trying to remember. When in a very relaxed state it is information that is received, or heard, within. You may ask, "Well how do I know that it is not just my own thinking?" Because, it is not information that is reached for, it is just allowed or received. This process of hearing with the inner ear usually takes quite a bit of training and confirmation. It requires time and training because in order for this type of communication to be effective, you need to develop a certain level of trust that you are receiving information from a source outside of yourself, and not just making things up. Building that kind of trust takes some time and it can be developed with training.

This "inner ear" type of communication is very common with psychics and mediums; often they hear spirits with their inner ear. They begin to develop this skill when they realize other people are not hearing what they are hearing. Like I mentioned before, it takes some training to develop the trust needed to affectively work with the inner ear.

#6 Audibly With the "Outer Ear"

Lastly we have audible communication with your Spirit Guides. This is just like it sounds only worse! When you hear your Spirit Guide audibly, you can hear them just like you hear someone talking to you, only their voice is usually louder, crisper and more startling. See, when tone or sound travels between dimensions, it comes through with a very unique sound. It is very crisp to your eardrum and you immediately identify it as something you have not heard before. This is your Spirit Guide's least favorite way to communicate with you for all of these reasons.

To give you an idea of what it is like, I will tell you about the first audible experience that I had with my Spirit Guide. Many years ago, when I was very young, I was in a large department store shopping by myself. During this time of my life, my family and I were in the midst of dealing with a very unstable family member. Needless to say, it was very difficult, and it was definitely taking a toll on everyone. While shopping, out of nowhere, I heard the most authoritative voice say, "Get out now!" The voice was so loud and crisp that I was frozen in my tracks. I couldn't breathe, my heart began to race like someone was chasing me, and my legs felt like concrete so I couldn't move. I looked behind me because it sounded as if the voice had come from someone standing directly behind me. I was scared to turn around, but as I did, I realized no one was there. So I looked around, and at the door, but to my surprise, everyone seemed fine. There was no urgency at all! I immediately got my bearings after what felt like ten very long minutes (but in actuality was probably about twenty seconds), and realized from the tone of the voice that it was not a person, but my Spirit Guide. Still terrified, I was looking around to see what could be so dangerous that I had to get out! Was there going to be a robbery? What was happening? When my eyes scanned the front door for the second time, I saw the troubled family member entering the store. This may not seem like a big deal to others, but at the time, the stress I was under was affecting my health, so I was very grateful to have avoided this encounter.

Now to be fair, I have also heard Frank audibly, like I would hear a regular person talking to me. However, because I have had previous experience with this type of communication, I knew immediately from the tone that it was a Spirit Guide. During the encounter in the department store, my guide was trying to contact me in an urgent way, so I would be more apt to listen, and not just blow it off, or not take the message seriously. With Frank the matter was not so urgent, so his voice was not as powerful. Because there was no sense of urgency in his voice, the tone was also not so loud. After the department store experience, however, I did ask my Spirit Guides not to scare the daylights out of me like that again. So now when they wish to talk with me audibly, they whisper or speak lightly as not to shock my system. I much prefer it that way.

Hearing your Spirit Guide audibly is not very common, even for psychics and mediums. In fact, I do not know many people at all who have heard their Spirit Guides this way. Most psychics and mediums receive information in some of the other forms that we have talked about, such as words, pictures, blocks of thought, or inner ear. So do not get discouraged if you have not heard or do not hear your Spirit Guides audibly; it is rare. In my opinion you might even want to be happy about not hearing them that way!

CHAPTER 4

WHAT IS IT LIKE TO RECEIVE COMMUNICATIONS FROM YOUR SPIRIT GUIDE?

I feel this is a very important step and it is often left out when you are learning about the spirit communication process. It is helpful when you know what it "feels" like to communicate with your Spirit Guide in order to help you develop your communication skills. When you become familiar with this process, then you better know what to expect when receiving information from them.

This is a really great time to give you some exercises to try.

Exercise #1
Observe the Alpha State

As you fall asleep at night, notice your relaxed mental state. When you find your mind wandering wildly and you begin to see dreamlike images in your mind's eye, you are in what is referred to as the Alpha state. Pay attention to what this Alpha state feels like whenever you go to sleep, and learn to recognize this state when you are meditating or during times of relaxation. Really observe the dreamlike images by allowing them in, do not force anything, observe the state of allowing, the state of no resistance. This is the key, relax and allow, relax and allow.

These Alpha experiences are very similar to what many mediums experience when communicating with spirits. When you do this exercise you will become familiar with the state that you will experience when communicating with spirits. During this time, you naturally let your guard down as you are preparing yourself to be spiritually aligned, through sleep. As part of the process you allow pictures to come in, with no resistance. This is an ability everyone has; it is just that not many people realize how useful it is. By doing this exercise you will become consciously aware of what it is like to receive and recognize the faint mental impressions that occur during spirit communication. You will become very aware of the state of allowing, with no attachments to what is coming in and what is going out. You should do this every night until you begin to feel the resistance to spirit communication diminish during your waking hours.

Exercise #2
Visualizing In the "Mind's Eye"

As we talked about before, your Spirit Guide's first and favorite choice of communication is through visions and words, via telepathy. So I would like you to read this and then do the exercise.

You see through your mind's eye all of the time, you probably just called it remembering. Remembering uses the same process of seeing in your "mind's eye." What you are "seeing" is what separates a memory from spirit communication. When you remember something you are seeing something in your mind's eye that you were a part of, hence, have a memory of; in other words, you were there so you remember it. When a Spirit Guide is trying to communicate with you through telepathy or your "mind's eye," you see it as if you remember it, only you never had that particular experience to remember. So it is new information that you see through the "mind's eye."

To practice this process, I want you to visualize something in your mind's eye. It could be a person or an object like a four leaf clover. Think of something and then close your eyes and concentrate for a few seconds on this image. See it and observe it, the color, the shape, and the size.

Then I want you to imagine seeing a red rose. I want you to look at it and observe it, the vivid color, the shape, and the size. See the thorns and observe how they would hurt if you touch them. Then I want you to touch the pedals of the rose, feel the softness, and observe how they feel like velvet. The next thing that I want you to do is to smell the rose, smell how strong the aroma is. I would like you to spend a few minutes observing the flower with all of your senses.

Then lastly, picture in your mind somewhere that you have always wanted to visit. Anywhere in the world, even if you are scared to go there, just imagine that you are there right now. Look around, what do you see? Are there people? Are you outside or inside? What do you hear? What do you smell? Spend some time at this place, seeing, hearing, smelling, and observing with all of your senses.

The purpose of this exercise is it helps you to become familiar with how it "feels" to see things in the mind's eye. These exercises are also designed to be a part of the training process for your "etheric" body, or spiritual body. The same way you exercise and train your physical body for something physical, you must also exercise and train your spiritual body in order to help you perform spiritual tasks as well.

Exercise #3
Hearing With Your "Inner Ear"

This exercise is going to be similar to the prior exercise. I also want you to read through this exercise before you try it.

Hearing with the inner ear is going to be very similar to seeing with the mind's eye. You have done this many times before through your memory, only instead of seeing something, it involves hearing something. Since I have explained the similarities once before, I am going to get right into the exercise. I want you to remember the last conversation that you had; what did the other person say? What did you say? Hear the tone of the conversation, hear the emotion, and observe what was said.

The next thing I would like you to do is to try and remember a song you have recently heard on the radio. Listen to it, hear the beat, hear the words, and enjoy the music. Let this song play for a while. Practice this exercise with different things, you can even do it with rain or wind or the sound of the ocean. Observe this state and what it feels like to hear with the inner ear. Become familiar with it.

Now that you have observed the Alpha state, seeing with your mind's eye and hearing with the inner ear, you can have a better understanding of the way in which Spirit Guides will often show you something, and you will have a better understanding of how spirit communication works. Now that you have a better understanding of this process and how it works, you can hone these skills so that they become quite affective.

Just remember that when you are first learning the communication process, however, the communication will most likely seem very light and subtle or even faint. When this happens it may feel a little difficult at first and this leaves some people feeling frustrated. But please note that this is a process. You have spent many, many years trying to block out any spirit communication. So you have to learn to tear down the very wall you have spent much time and many years building. However, as your sensitivity begins to develop again, as it will if you are consistent, these messages will seem anything but subtle. It takes time, so be patient. I worked on developing strong spirit communication skills for close to five years when I was young and I am a psychic! But I was very focused on becoming the best spirit communicator that I could be!

CHAPTER 5

CHAKRAS AND SPIRIT COMMUNICATION

*H*ere is an area where I feel most people fail when teaching about spirit communication. They either forget about it, assume you know it (big mistake), or they truly don't understand the correlation themselves between the chakra system and spirit communication as teachers. Your chakra system is a very important part of the spirit communication system. It is vital for you to pay attention to and understand your chakra system when you are developing spirit communication. If you know about chakras already, DO NOT skip over this section, as 99 percent of people do not actually know where their chakra systems lie, and this is important for you to know.

However, I am going to quickly run over the basics first. What is your chakra system? It is energy centers where your physical body and your etheric body meet. Your etheric body is your "spiritual body." You have seven main chakras on the body and they each do different things. See diagram below:

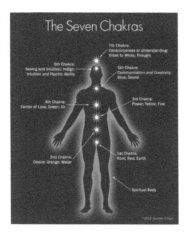

Now, even I did not realize myself until I started teaching spirit communication classes that most people do not know where their chakras centers are on their own body. As you can see from the diagram, the chakra system is right down the center of the body, which is correct; however, the chakra centers themselves do not lie in the center of your body (front to back) but they are actually near your back or near your spine. Most people see the diagrams and/or have read things that say they are down the center of the body, and assume this also means of equal distance from the front of your body as well as from the back of your body. Many people believe the chakra system starts at the center of the top of your head and extends down through the center of the body, and this is not where the meeting point is (where your physical and etheric body meet). The chakras do extend out to the center of your body and even beyond, but the meeting point is located near your spinal column. Why is this important? Because you will utilize the chakra system during spirit communication; in fact, it is an important component in the process. Primarily you will be working with chakras four, five, and six, and this meeting point is something with which

25

you will become very familiar during this process. It is also very important to developing your sensitivity level and learning control as you advance.

Since this is not a book about the chakra system I am only going to briefly touch upon them, in order to give you the information that you need. Chakra is "Sanskrit" for wheel or disk. They are spinning wheels of energy, or "vortexes." They filter energy from the environment and allow only matching vibrations in and rid the rest. It is where psychic energy travels from the spirit realm to you in the physical realm. There are seven main chakra centers and they are each responsible for different things in your spiritual and physical bodies. Each of them is also represented by a color.

1st Chakra
Root Chakra (Color: Red)

- Earth chakra, it is your foundation
- Glands: adrenals
- Other Body Parts: legs, feet, bones, large intestine, teeth
- Malfunction: weight problems, hemorrhoids, constipation, sciatica, degenerative arthritis, knee troubles
- Survival chakra
- Purpose: to ground you like a lightning rod (very important in spiritual work), plugs your energy into the earth's energy. Grounding is a coping mechanism for stress.

2nd Chakra
Desire Chakra (Color: Orange)

- Water chakra

- Glands: ovaries, testicles
- Body Parts: womb, genitals, kidney, bladder, circulatory system
- Malfunction: impotence, frigidity, uterine, bladder or kidney trouble, stiff lower back
- Purpose: to let go and flow (movement). The center of sexuality, emotions, desire, sensation, pleasure, movement and nurturance. Related to the moon and its pull on energy.
- Clairsentience/empath is the psychic sense of the second chakra

3rd Chakra
Power Chakra (Color: Yellow)

- Fire chakra
- Glands: pancreas, adrenals
- Body Parts: digestive system, muscles
- Malfunction: ulcers, diabetes, hypoglycemia, digestive disorders
- Intuition sits in this chakra—gut feeling
- Purpose: transformation and personal power

4th Chakra
The Center of Love (Color: Green)

- Air chakra
- Glands: thymus
- Body Parts: lungs, heart, pericardium, arms, hands
- Malfunctions: asthma, high blood pressure, heart disease, lung disease
- Purpose: compassion and love
- Higher consciousness elevates and expands the heart chakra; therefore, it is sometimes utilized

during spirit communication. Empaths also utilize this chakra.

5th Chakra
Communication/Creativity Chakra (Color: Blue)

- Sound chakra
- Glands: thyroid, parathyroid
- Body Parts: neck, shoulders, arms, hands
- Malfunction: sore throat, stiff neck, colds, thyroid problems, hearing problems
- Purpose: communication and creativity, communication through sound, vibration, self-expression, and creativity. It includes listening, speaking, writing, telepathy and any of the arts. As your creative chakra, artists and musicians utilize this chakra consistently.
- Channeling information from the spirit realm, channels utilize this chakra almost always during spirit communication.

6th Chakra
Seeing and Intuition (Color: Indigo)

- Intuition and psychic ability chakra
- Glands: pineal
- Body Parts: eyes
- Malfunction: blindness, headaches, nightmares, eyestrain, blurred vision
- Purpose: development of psychic abilities
- Clairvoyance or clear seeing

7th Chakra
Consciousness or Understanding Chakra

(Color: Violet to White)

- Thought chakra
- Gland: pituitary
- Body Parts: cerebral cortex, central nervous system
- Malfunctions: depression, alienation, confusion, boredom, apathy, inability to learn
- Purpose: this chakra is the seat of enlightenment
- The function is thought and knowing or claircognizance

So now that you know the basics, you need to pay particular attention to chakras four, five, and six. Those are the ones in between the shoulder blades, the upper back and back of your neck, and back of your head. Why? Because when you are working with spirit communication those chakras open and they open wide!

When I first really started to develop my spirit communication to an advanced level, something really threw me off. I would be walking around constantly feeling like there was a huge gapping hole in the back of my neck and sometimes I could feel a hole between my shoulder blades as well. I could tell that they were clearly two different holes; they did not run into each other and they felt very separate to me. They felt so big it seemed as if someone could put a fist in there. The weird thing was that I knew there was no hole, so what was going on? Well, most teachers do not teach about this particular experience because they do not know themselves, or they assume and take for granted that you know what this big gapping hole is. But in either case this is the "meeting point" which I mentioned earlier; this is the place where your two bodies meet. The feeling is your chakra centers opening wide and activating to allow information to be received from the spiritual realm and your spiritual body and transferring this information to your physical body. When you become more advanced you can learn to open and close those centers at will, but when you are first developing you may walk around feeling "open" in the back. They will activate at random and it can be really annoying when you are at the movie theater! You can feel this "opening" behind your head, neck, or between your shoulder blades. You could feel them open all at once, or it could be one at a time, it makes no difference. The way that they open and which ones open at what time is unique to each individual.

Something else you might experience, besides the energetic gapping holes in your back (as if that is not enough), is when your fifth or sixth chakra begins to activate, you may also start to heat up. Channels experience this sensation often when they communicate with spirits. What do I mean by heat up? Well, usually around your ears you will become very hot and tingly. You will feel heat stemming from the inside of your being, and your skin will become red to reflect the heat. You will also feel hot to the touch. I am a natural channel, not just a psychic, so this is something that I experience. This was also new to me when it first began to happen. When I am working with spirits, I begin to feel the heat first and then the hole, but the heat seems to precede the feeling of the hole. The heat starts around the back of my neck or ears and as I continue to raise my vibration, I begin to turn red from the heat. My ears heat up so hot that people say it feels like I am burning up. When I am really heating up it will run from my ears all the way down my neck. At first, when I was young, it weirded me out! I couldn't figure out why I was getting so hot, especially because developing your skills happens at random, not just during spirit communication. Now that I am more skilled in the process, I have total control; I can raise my vibration and open those centers at will and close them down at will. Now I enjoy it; I become very relaxed when I start to heat up. I am in what people in sports call a "zone." Heat is a very good indicator of a channeling ability. I have heated up so much from writing this book right now you could probably fry an egg on my neck… but I am not going to confirm it!

CHAPTER 6

10 TIPS FOR WORKING WITH SPIRIT GUIDES AND SPIRITS

This section is going to contain a list of ten simple tips to help you when you are learning to develop your Spirit Guide communication. These are important and though they are in no particular order, they are equally important!

Tip #1
Know Who You Are Working With

When you begin to work on developing your Spirit Guide communication, you are opening the door to the spirit world so you will naturally open the door to other spirits as well. This is something that is important for you to have knowledge about and something you should be aware of. If you are not aware of this, you could receive information from spirits who are *not* your Spirit Guide. Even spirits who do not have your best interest at heart; yes, as much as I never wanted to believe in bad intentioned spirits, it is true, it can happen! This is why you should never, ever, play with a

Ouija board. To avoid working with spirits who are not your Spirit Guide, there are a few things you should know to help you tell the difference, as well as steps you should take to specifically ask for the spirit contact to be with your Spirit Guide or spirits of the highest vibration. That being said, I will give you some simple steps to help you avoid attracting undesirables.

Tip #2
Say a Prayer First

When you are trying to contact or connect with your Spirit Guide, always, always say a prayer first and ask for only the highest vibration of spirits who are working for your greatest good to come through. Something along the lines of, "I would like to make contact with my Spirit Guide, I am asking for my Spirit Guide to come in and make contact with me. Only the highest vibration of spirits are allowed to make contact with me, those who come from the white light of the Holy Spirit, amen," or, "I would only like to speak with my Spirit Guide, who comes with the highest vibration and from the white light of the Holy Spirit, all other spirits are not allowed to make contact with me." You get the idea.

Tip #3
Spirits Are Attracted To Us When We Think Of Them

Yes, it is true, when you think of a spirit they tend to come in. So if you feel a spirit around you during a meditation, you can ask them to show themselves to you or ask them if they have any messages for you and just feel their presence. When you ask them a question, make sure to stay in the state of allowing, in order for the pictures to come in.

If there are no pictures, then just feel their presence and enjoy the feeling of them making themselves known to you on the physical plane. Feeling their presence does just as much as allowing as far as strengthening the connection. For example, if you see a spirit in your mind's eye, use all of your senses. Feel them, allow the vision of them to form, and listen to hear if they are saying anything. Spirits are attracted to you when you think of them because when you think of them, it is like you are calling for them. They hear the call in the spiritual realm and they come to you. This is also why it is very common for you to feel loved ones who have passed over when you are thinking of them. If you are thinking of someone and feel their presence, close your eyes and just concentrate on that feeling, just feel them. Then allow any pictures to float in and out with no judgment, because they may try to tell you something. Many times it is just that they love you or they are watching over you, something along those lines. They do not give you lotto numbers!

Tip #4
Spirit Guides Do Not Come To You or Present Themselves To You With Physical Disabilities

Generally spirits in the spirit world do not have any physical disabilities they may have had here on earth. If you see a spirit who is deformed or you perceive them as angry, confused, or unhappy, you may be encountering an earth bound spirit or what people like to call a ghost. When you are learning to develop your spirit communication skills, it is wise to avoid contact with such spirits. If you encounter a spirit who makes you uncomfortable, you should repeat the prayer for protection, a prayer like I mentioned in tip #2, until you feel them leave or you feel comfortable. Also, imagine a barrier of white light surrounding you that only the highest vibration spirits can penetrate. Lastly ask for your Angels to come in, and remove any low vibration spirits from your area and take them away. After your Angels come in, the uncomfortable spirit should be gone. When you become more experienced and advanced in communicating with spirits, you may want to try to help earth bound spirits by encouraging them to go to the white light so that they can transition to the "Other Side." You can ask for Angles or loved ones to come in to try and help them make the transition. There is also a process of explaining to them that they are no longer physically alive, but for now, it is good just to concentrate on working with your Spirit Guide.

Tip #5
Write Things/Experiences Down

It is a good practice for you to write down all of your experiences afterwards. Often, you may find that a message will become clearer when you write it down. During the moment you are receiving information you are in the process of allowing, or in a state of no resistance. When you are doing this, you are working more with the right brain. When you write things down, you will switch into a different mode of remembering and analyzing; this is where you will switch from right brain to left brain. When you make this transition from right brain to left brain, sometimes it can help you to remember things or little details you may have missed otherwise. Write your experiences down as if you are writing a letter to someone else. Explain your experience in great detail so when you read it later, you can recall the experience more vividly. During this writing process you may actually receive even more information and sometimes it can turn into an automatic writing session without you even being aware of it. This process allows you to move from right brain to left brain more fluidly because you are still tuned into the spirit realm and you are not so focused on your belief system. So when you begin to write, your barriers are already down. All kinds of amazing information can come through this way (I have an exercise for this coming up).

Tip #6
Never Do Anything You Would Not Normally Do

What I mean by this is exactly what it says; never do anything that you would not otherwise do because you think a spirit told you to do it, or that you are being "guided" in some way. Spirits do not usually "tell" you to do something in particular. They will not tell you that you should get a divorce or make an investment of some kind. When you are communicating with your Spirit Guide it is more like they are showing you what path is best to take and why. You are meant to receive this information, weigh it with all the other knowledge you have, and then make a decision. Your Spirit Guide's role is to help you consider all things physical and spiritual before guiding you towards a decision. They are here to offer you spiritual guidance; their job is not to be a dictator. View it as more of a joint collaboration than being told what to do. Low vibration spirits, on the other hand, can and in some instances will try to influence you into making a certain decision; decisions which are meant to cause you issues or problems. Low vibration spirits can have bad intentions. In the beginning you may have difficulty distinguishing your Spirit Guide from other spirits. So if the information feels good and right in your heart, then it is pretty safe to say it is good information. If it just doesn't feel right, then don't jump into anything without further consideration.

Tip #7
Physical Sensations Are Common

You may feel physical sensations around your head, neck, ears, back, or in other parts of your body. This can be an indication of your Spirit Guides working with healing energy to give you a healing or working on your electromagnetic system in order to help you become more sensitive to receive spirit communications. The interesting thing is that these sensations usually come after or between working on your spirit communication and development, instead of during (besides the heating up that I talked about in the chakra chapter). Some of these sensations can include things like:

- Tingling Sensation
- Prickly Sensation
- Feeling Hot/Cold
- Hot Spots

Assuming that you have a clean bill of health, if you are working on developing your spirit communication skills, these things can be common. What confuses people is that these sensations can occur at any time, and it's not usually during spirit contact. A couple of these things used to happen to me when I was younger and working hard on my own communication skills. I used to get a prickly hot and cold feeling all over my body, for a while I thought it was a sign of dehydration. But, I drank lots of water and had regular checkups, and physically I was fine. These prickly sensations would usually last about one to two hours and go away. At the time, I would also usually have a "knowing" or visions of being worked on energetically by my Spirit Guides. It seemed as if my electrical system, or electromagnetic system, was being rewired, and in an odd way, that's what it felt like. This would usually last a couple of days then disappear for several months. I do not get them anymore. Another thing that would happen is, I would get hot spots all over my body, accompanied with the same visions. It felt like someone was holding a lighter to my skin, only from the inside. I would have many of these hot spots going on at one time all over my body. They didn't hurt, but it was really annoying! Why does this happen? It's like I mentioned before, when you are truly committed to working with your Spirit Guides, your physical system usually needs some adjustment. So your Spirit Guides work with your inner "electrical" system in order to make it possible for you to raise your vibration to a very high level. Imagine that you have an old electrical system in your house and you rewire it so you can install a whole new communication system; it's like that. If this does happen to you, you will know, because it feels like it sounds, like you are being rewired! Don't worry about it though, it doesn't hurt, it's just a strange feeling.

Tip #8
Be Consistent

If you really want to develop your ability to work with your Spirit Guides, consistency is the key! Can you develop this ability without consistency? Yes; however, it takes longer and you will not become as advanced. When I say consistent, I do not mean it has to disrupt your daily routine, simply make it a part of your daily routine. In other words, make it part of your morning ritual or nighttime ritual or both. I used to do my Spirit Guide communication meditation every morning for about two years straight. I would get up an extra twenty to thirty minutes early, take a shower, eat, get ready, then use the extra time I had to do the meditation. I began to enjoy it very much. Starting my day this way made a difference on how I felt; I felt calmer, and I began to see a correlation between meditation in the morning and my day going smoother. On the days I didn't do the meditation, things seemed to be a little more jumbled, and things didn't seem to go as smooth, so I got to the point where I really looked forward to it. I tried to do it every day, but obviously that is hard to do, so I was happy if I could do it five times a week. What consistency does is it sets a time when your Spirit Guide knows you are looking for them. Plus, it regulates your brainwave pattern making it easier to go into the Alpha state quicker. You do not have to do the Spirit Guide meditation every day; alternately, you could do the writing exercise (which I include in the exercise portion).

Tip #9
Meditation

If you choose to go the writing route to further develop your spirit communication skills, tip #9 is very, very important. Just to be clear, I want to tell you exactly what meditation is and why you need to do it (like I said before, I want to cover all bases). Meditation is a practice of sitting quietly, while regulating your breath using intone mantras or visualization in attempts to harmonize your mind, body, and soul. Why is this important? Well, because meditation is really effective in clearing out mind clutter as well as energetic clutter. It is knocking out two birds with one stone, so to speak, on a spiritual and physical level.

You clean your house, take showers, eat right, and maintain your physical health by getting the proper rest, etcetera.

Well, it is equally important to your physical and spiritual health to keep your mind and your energetic field as clutter free as possible. This will allow you to operate at your most efficient level.

There have been some extensive studies done on meditation and the most noteworthy finding of these studies seemed to show in the EEG measuring of brain wave patterns. During your waking consciousness, brain waves are random and chaotic. The brain usually operates with different wavelengths from the front to the back of the brain, and from hemisphere to hemisphere. Meditation changes this drastically. Subjects in meditation show increased Alpha waves and these waves continue to increase throughout the duration of the meditation. Also, the front and the back of the brain begin to synchronize as well as the left and the right hemispheres. In other words, the different areas of your brain begin to work together synchronistically! There has been documented research, which shows that the daily practice of meditation creates a more efficient, integrated brain functioning. After a few months, this integration in the brain is not just noticed during the meditation state but during daily activity as well. I can personally attest to this, as it helped me learn how to go into the Alpha state quickly, and at will, for when I do psychic readings.

Health wise, meditation has also been linked to lowering blood pressure, helping with anxiety and depression just to name a few. Not to mention the spiritual aspects of raising your vibration, intuitive development and raising your consciousness.

Here is a meditation exercise I designed to help you work more efficiently with the Universal Laws. I suggest doing some type of meditation at least once a day, I personally recommend for you to do it in the morning if you only have time for one meditation. Morning meditation, I have noticed, definitely sets the tone of your day.

Meditation Exercise

Before you begin, find a quiet place where you will not be disturbed. You will be using a chair for this meditation, so find a comfortable chair to sit in, then place both feet flat on the floor.

1) Define what it is that you want to achieve in your meditation. This is a very important step whether it is calmness, joy, better health, or happiness; whatever it is that you desire. This is very important because intent is what actually creates things whether it is in the Spiritual or Physical realm.

2) Sit comfortably in a chair or in an upright position in a quiet place.

3) Close your eyes and concentrate on your breathing. Slow your breathing to a relaxed state.

4) When your breathing is rhythmic, concentrate on relaxing all of the muscles in your body.

5) Imagine that your spine is like a string on a musical instrument. Imagine that this string or cord attaches all of your chakras together, from your root chakra to your crown chakra.

6) Visualize this string or cord vibrating. Imagine that you are in control of how fast or slow the vibration is. Next raise this vibration to the highest level of vibration that you can achieve.

7) When you are vibrating at a high level, imagine that you can see a river above your body. Imagine that this river is the river of the Universe. This river of the Universe contains all the Universal energy.

8) Then visualize that you are attaching your energy to the Universal River. When you attach your energy with the

Universal River, feel yourself flowing in harmony with the Universal Laws.

9) From that state imagine whatever it is that you desire being attracted to you. Imagine that your desires are coming to you as if you are a human magnet.

10) Remain in this state until you feel a sense of completion, and then release this image into the Universe.

You should not set a time limit on how long or short your meditation should be, just do what feels right. For many people it will change each day, some days it might be twenty minutes while others it might be two minutes. The consistency of meditation (how many times a week, etcetera) is more important than how long the meditation is. In my opinion, meditation time should be adjusted to fit your own personal needs depending on what is happening in your life at the time.

Tip #10
Be Patient!

This is the one tip I think people struggle with the most: being patient. Like I said before, I spent two years consistently working on my spirit communication development and doing the Spirit Guide communication meditation at least four to five times a week. I spent three more years advancing and developing that skill to the best of my ability, a total of five years! Not to mention spirit communication is what I do for a living, so I practice my skill for many, many hours every single day. Does that mean you have to do what I did or do now? Absolutely not! Unless, of course, you want to tell other people what their Spirit Guides wish them to know, or what Grandma has to say, for a living. But do not try this a few times and think, "This doesn't work!" You need to be committed and realistic, and know it's a process. It's not easy what I do; if everyone did it, there would be no need for psychics or mediums. In other words, it's like anything else: if you want to learn to play golf, you take lessons and you practice. If you want to learn to surf, you take lessons and you practice. If you want to learn to ski, you take lessons and you practice. You get the point!

CHAPTER 7

COMMUNICATING WITH SPIRIT GUIDES
THROUGH WRITING

*U*tilizing writing techniques as a means of developing your spirit communication is a way of channeling your Spirit Guides or higher self that is not so scary, as well as utilizing your left and right brains which can be more comfortable for some people. It is a process of allowing them to speak through you in blocks of thought, the mind's eye, inner ear, or whatever works, through writing it down instead of speaking it. This practice is very effective because people get caught up in getting their "ideas" or channeled information down on paper or on the computer instead of analyzing where it is coming from. There are a few different ways you can do this. One way is through automatic writing. Many great books have been written this way; in fact, I wrote large portions of my book *Soul DNA* this way. I would sit at the computer and go okay, what information do you have for me today? Then after a few minutes it would just start coming in. It would come in so fast that I did not even have a chance to read it. I would just write and write for hours. Then I would read it later and think, "Wow, this is great stuff!" Many people write songs this way, or poems; it's a wonderful tool and effective when utilized. This first exercise is to learn how to develop your automatic writing skill.

Exercise #1
Automatic Writing

1) Sit down with the intention of writing about anything you are spiritually interested in, or about something that is important in your life, such as problems you might be having that you would like to address.

2) As always, you should start any Spirit Guide communication process with a prayer asking for only the highest vibration spirits to be allowed to make contact with you, only spirits who come from the white light of the Holy Spirit. Then you want to imagine a white light coming down from above and surrounding you and protecting you from any low entity spirits.

3) After you prepare yourself, you can begin writing, on paper or at a keyboard. Start by thinking of a question then remove yourself and allow yourself to answer from an "outsider's perspective." As you begin this outsider view, it allows you to remove your own beliefs and tap into the spirit world by allowing new information to come through you in your writing. This detachment is a learning process; however, once you get in the habit of it and know what it "feels" like, you will be able to do it at will. It takes a little while to develop a skill in automatic writing; it can take months and sometimes years, so do not get impatient. But if you like to write, it is well worth it!

4) When you get into the flow of writing, do not stop and read it or edit it. Continue to write all of the information that comes into your mind until you feel the flow stop, or until you need a break. If you try and stop to read it, this will shift you from right brain to left brain and puts a hiccup in

the process. It will then take some time to reestablish the flow. Allow the process to flow naturally until it is done.

5) When you become "tuned in" while writing, normally you will have some physical sensations. They may seem very subtle at first, but they will become stronger as you develop. You will become very relaxed; the feeling is very similar to being in a meditative state. You may also feel hot or begin to turn red as your chakras start to open. Writing is a form of channeling, so this is very common. Pay close attention to any physical sensations you have when practicing any spirit communication exercises. If you pay attention, sometimes you will feel the physical sensations come first, then you will know that your body is preparing itself for spirit communication.

6) This process is a development process, so remember that you will have to put in some time writing in order to see results. If you enjoy writing, excellent! If you do not enjoy writing and you just want to advance in spirit communication, do not force yourself to do this. There are all kinds of ways to advance, which I am covering in this book. You do not need to do all of the exercises here in this book; in fact, I do not even recommend it. You should just do the ones that suit you best, or that you are most interested in.

CHAPTER 8

SPIRIT GUIDES COMMUNICATION
THROUGH DREAMING

*D*reaming is actually one of the easiest, most natural ways to connect with the spirit world. For over fifty years scientists have continued to study the science behind dreaming. The only really, really solid reason they have come up with for the reason behind why we dream is because we get sleepy! It has had scientists baffled for years, and will continue to do so, as they are not looking for the answers they are seeking in the right place. They have failed to study dreaming/sleeping from a spiritual aspect, as they are scientists, studying from the physical side. From a physical perspective they have proven that we get enough rest during the day from sitting at our desks, driving our cars, and sitting while watching TV, that sleep is not required for our physical body.

It is, however, required for our spiritual health. We have been programmed through our Soul DNA, or spiritual genetic system, to spiritually align ourselves every single day, and it's called sleep. Sleep is how we spiritually align ourselves. What is spiritual alignment? It is a time in which we break away from the physical realm and its limitations, to explore other dimensions, other realities, and become spiritually free with no limitations. We astral travel, we have complete access to the spirit world, and we reach higher consciousness. It is, and should be, viewed as an extension of your reality. Nowadays, you are told from a very young age that your dreams are like a fantasy or something that does not exist. Eventually, you start to believe this information as fact, that dreaming is not a reality. For the last five hundred years or so, dreaming has very much been viewed as useless; it is just something you do each night between "real life." But it has not always been this way. In fact, it used to be very different!

Dreaming is something that has been embraced a lot more in history than it is now. Dreaming is taken for granted in the modern world, mostly because of people's lack of understanding, and the knowledge behind why we dream having been lost and/or forgotten. Ancient civilizations had a great understanding of why we dream, and they used to revolve their everyday lives around what they would see in their dreams. In fact, it was very important in helping them function. Dreams were found recorded on clay tablets dating back to around 4000—3000 BC. Ancient civilizations didn't see dreaming as just something you do while you sleep, they actually saw it as an extension of our reality. They didn't seem to try and separate the differences between real life and dreaming but instead molded them together as one and lived their lives this way. Romans and Greeks are great examples on how big of an impact dreams had on their lives. They believed that dreams were direct messages from the Gods forewarning them about future events, or advice and guidance of what they should do. It was seen as a religious morale to listen to your dreams and was highly encouraged. They would not only listen to their dreams, but they would look at them as guidance. They would look into their dreams for answers to problems they were having. For example, before technology was invented to help diagnose a sickness, or help determine what medicine you should take, people would instead look to their dreams for answers on what was wrong with them, and how to heal themselves.

There were also dream analysts that people could go to if they didn't understand their dreams. The dream analysts would analyze the dream for you and give you the messages behind your dreams. Dream analysts were looked up to and highly respected. They were usually a big part of the decision making process for the government or the military. Military leaders would use them to help with tactics in order to defeat their enemies. In the Hellenistic times in Greece, they built temples called Asclepieions, where sick people would go and sleep, and the cures would be given to them via dreams.

Ancient Chinese and Mexican civilizations believed that your spirit would actually leave your body while you were dreaming and it would wander to other places. They believed that if you were to awaken while your body was in a deep sleep, and your spirit was wandering, that it would not find its way back to the body, therefore, you would die. Some cultures still look down upon alarm clocks, for fear of suddenly being woken up. They also believed they were able to speak to their ancestors through their dreams, and that their ancestors were made up of different objects or parts of nature in the dreams, but their spirit was in them. As you can see, dreams had a huge impact on people's lives back in history, and many of them had the same theory of being guided and warned of events in the waking life. However, dreaming was not always looked at as something positive. During the middle ages people looked at dreams as horrible tricks. People believed that while you where dreaming, the devil was tempting you with certain images and temptations in your most vulnerable state. Therefore, they did not embrace dreams, and basically had the exact opposite understanding of them than more ancient civilizations. Now, when you get into more modern times, scientists started doing tests on the brain and body while you're in a dreaming state and found that there is a lot more brain activity going on than when you're awake.

It seems like now people are so sidetracked by technology and materials that they have lost interest in one of the most amazing abilities that they have. The ability to spiritually align yourself and shift dimensions while being able to maintain a physical existence!

So now that you have a better understand of what dreaming actually is – an extension of your reality – and that it also naturally allows you very easy access into the spirit world, I am going to give you another exercise. I am sure you have heard of this exercise before, it is called dream journaling.

Exercise #2
Dream Journaling

Why dream journaling? Because this is the first step in helping you to remember your dreams, even if you do not think that you dream. Secondly, it will allow you to become more familiar with this "other reality" and the other dimensions that you visit. When you become more aware of these things, and you realize on a waking consciousness level that other realities exist and other experiences with the consciousness are possible, then you activate certain potentials within yourself. It alters electromagnetic connections both within the mind, brain, and even perceptive mechanisms. These things will then bring together reservoirs of energy allowing the waking conscious mind to increase its sensitivity. This allows you to no longer be afraid of other realities, which is a huge step in letting your resistance down in order to develop spirit communication. Lastly, it will help you to learn how to analyze what information you are receiving from the spirit world or your Spirit Guides. You are very susceptible to receiving very valid information during your dream state from your Spirit Guides as you have just learned from our little history lesson.

1) First you should pick a good dream journal and leave it by your bed. Pick something that you like, try not to just throw a few sheets of paper over there, unless that's all you have at the moment. A journal specifically picked to be your dream journal helps to keep everything in order and not be cluttered with other things like shopping lists, etcetera. Also, make sure that you have something to write with. I don't want you searching around for something to write with in the morning.

2) This is very *important*: always write in your dream journal first thing in the morning. You are still in a groggy state when you wake up, and you are still tapped into your higher consciousness, so this is when you can really get some great information. The later in the day it gets, the foggier the dream becomes and it makes it very hard to remember all of the details.

3) Try to write something in your dream journal every day for two months. Even if it's something short that seems insignificant. The reason for this is, many times writing will jog your memory of other things that happened during the dream state. It is also during these two months that you are honing in this new skill.

4) Ask for guidance before you fall asleep. Talk to your Spirit Guide and ask them for their guidance. Ask them to help you with a specific problem at work, a personal issue, or whatever it is that you are stressed about. Do not get frustrated if you do not "dream" your solution right away. This is

a training process; you are shifting your perspective on why you dream, and training yourself to utilize dreaming more effectively. This takes time. Your belief system has been in place for many, many years; with the perspective that dreaming was not even useful. This belief has allowed many people to block dreaming from their memory, as insignificant to their life. When you realize it actually is an extension of your reality with the potential to help you to receive much needed guidance, it can also be a little bit of added pressure.

5) Give each dream a name or title. This helps you to find dreams faster if you are searching for a specific one later. It also allows you to sum up the over all "feel" of the experience you are going to be writing down. It's like giving a title to a story. Or in some instances just by naming the dream or giving it a title can trigger an awareness of the overall meaning of the dream.

6) Put more emphasis on the "feel" of the dream than the actual dream itself. Write down symbols and all of that, but make sure you note how you felt throughout the dream; lost, confused, happy, concerned, etcetera. This theme on how you "feel" is repetitive when developing your spirit communication skills. Your sixth sense is felt in the body and throughout this entire process you are going to retrain yourself how to get back in touch with these senses. So, in essence, how you "feel" during the dream is just as important as everything else you can remember.

7) After writing down your dream, look at your dream from an outsider's perspective, like you learned to do during the automatic writing exercise. View it from outside of yourself and try and form an overall picture of what the dream means with no attachment. Try and connect the dots; if you are scared of something and you dream about it, then you are probably facing something during your waking conscious state that you are scared of. For instance, I used to be scared

of tornados, so when I was really stressed out I would dream about them. If I was just a little stressed, I would dream about one or two tornados. However, if I was really stressed out, I would dream about six or seven of them, each one representing something different. When I dream about where I am on my life path, I will dream about roads. Such as where I am on the road, if I am lost on the road, etcetera.

If you do this exercise for a while, slowly you will be able to receive information from your Spirit Guide via dreaming. However, like I mentioned before, be persistent and patient. I worked on this for about a year before I got really, really good at it.

CHAPTER 9

SPIRIT GUIDE COMMUNICATION MEDITATION

*T*his is a process I strongly recommend, and it seems to be the most popular one, it is a called Spirit Guide Communication Meditation. This is a meditation specifically created and geared towards helping you learn to make contact with your Spirit Guide and help you to become more aware of the sensations or "feelings" when in the presence of your Spirit Guide. This is different than doing a regular meditation, because it has the specific purpose to help you with spirit communication. Here's what you do:

Exercise #3
Spirit Guide Meditation

You can do this lying down on your bed or sitting comfortably in a chair. The best time to do this meditation (unlike your regular meditation) is usually at night before you go to sleep since you won't be interrupted. The veil is also thinner at night and it also helps to prepare you for sleep and interesting dreams.

1) Say a prayer and ask that only the highest vibration of spirits is allowed to make contact with you. Only spirits who come from the white light of the Holy Spirit are allowed in your space. Then see a white light come down from above, see the light surround your body until you are entirely engulfed in the white light. See this white light as a barrier against all other spirits that do not come from the white light of the Holy Spirit.

2) Close your eyes and relax. Relax all of your muscles, starting with your head, your neck, your shoulders, your arms, and your stomach. Feel all of your stress melt away... feel your hips relax, your thighs, your calves and your feet.

3) Imagine you are walking into an elevator and the doors close behind you. You are on the twentieth floor. See the buttons in front of you and push the button that says one. Feel the elevator begin to move, you are now on your way down. See the numbered display above the elevator doors, and notice that the light has moved from the number twenty to nineteen, as you feel the elevator going down. Continue to watch the lights move to eighteen then seventeen. Breathe deeply between floors. Next you see sixteen and so on. Feel the motion of the elevator as you continue to go down, watch the numbered lights counting down, and count them in your mind as you breathe deeply once or twice between floors. The elevator stops as you reach the first floor, and the doors open. Step out.

4) When you step out there is a path in front of you. This path is a bright yellow path of bricks. On each side of the path is green grass and large beautiful trees. It is sunny outside and there are colorful flowers. You can hear birds in the distance. Step onto the path and follow it along. You reach the bridge and continue across, you can hear the running water below; it is very soothing. Follow the path as it leads you up to a cottage. This cottage has a very beautiful

wood door with carvings in it. Look at the craftsmanship and admire its features.

5) When you are ready, go into the cottage, open the door, and walk in. In the middle of the room you will see two chairs, one is for you and one is for your Spirit Guide. The chairs have a high back and they are facing the other way, so you cannot see who is sitting in the chair. Walk around the chairs and see who is there. What do they look like? Are they male or female? Are they tall or short, dark hair or light hair? Is their hair short or long? How old are they? What are they wearing?

6) Have a conversation with them and ask them what they would like you to know. Then listen. Usually they will communicate with you by blocks of thought via telepathy; however, sometimes you can hear them with your "inner ear." What pictures are you seeing? What words are you seeing? Can you hear anything? Is there anyone else in the room? Do they want to talk with you? If so, ask what messages they have for you. They may also communicate with you by connecting with your claircognizance, and you will just "know" what message they are trying to convey.

7) Spend some time "feeling" what it is like to be in the presence of your Spirit Guide, even if you cannot see them completely. Even if you can just sense their presence, spend some time becoming familiar with how it feels. What sensations are you experiencing? Can you feel them behind you or in front of you? To which side of you do you feel them? Do you feel warm in their presence, or tingly? Do you feel your chakras opening? All of these sensations are important because you will become accustomed to feeling these sensations when your Spirit Guide is around. In fact, these sensations will begin to help you differentiate when you are thinking of something yourself or when your Spirit Guide is

trying to communicate a message to you. When you're receiving spirit communication, they will be accompanied by these sensations. That is how you will be able to tell the difference: if the messages are not accompanied by some type of physical sensation, then it is most likely your own great idea or note to self!

8) When you are done experiencing the presence of your Spirit Guide, thank them and exit the cottage. Make sure to close the door behind you. Follow the yellow brick path back over the bridge and to the elevator. Then step into the elevator and push the button for number twenty. The doors will close and you will begin to feel the elevator moving upward. Watch the numbers rise and light up as you move past the other floors. Floor one, two, three; take a nice deep breath between each floor as you feel the elevator moving up. Four, five, six, and so on until you reach floor twenty. The elevator will stop and the doors will open. Step out and open your eyes. You're done.

Now that you know how to get to your cottage, you can go back there any time and talk to whomever you find there. You can spend some time there and design the cottage in any way you wish. You can add windows, things to write on, furniture; whatever makes you feel comfortable and happy. When you become comfortable with the process, you might want to ask for help with a particular issue before going into the meditation, and see what answers come to you when you get to your cottage. The journey should feel relaxing and enjoyable. Sometimes when you work on developing your spirit communication through avenues such as this, you may even receive the answers in your dream state (which is similar to this meditative state). The insights on this journey are invaluable. The dreams you'll have after doing this exercise may be a little more clear than usual. Pay attention to them and what they might be trying to tell you. Make sure to write them in your dream journal.

*PLEASE NOTE: I've created a Spirit Guide Meditation here if you'd like to have one in audio. https://keystothespiritworld.com/product/spirit-guide-meditation

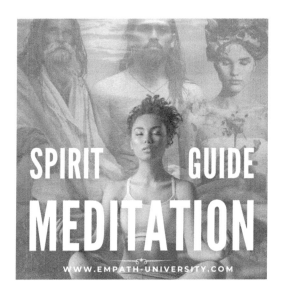

CHAPTER 10

5 COMMON "BLOCKS"

ou have learned a lot about spirit communication as well as many exercises to try. I am confident that you have learned enough to help you with a strong start. In closing, I wanted to address some issues, in case you find yourself running into some hang-ups along the way. So I went ahead and made a list of the most common blocks people encounter when learning to communicate with their Spirit Guide. What do I mean by blocks? It's just like it sounds, a list of five things that can keep you from being able to discover your ability to communicate and work with your Spirit Guide. I have also given solutions for each block, as I want you to have all of the tools that you need to make this a very satisfying journey.

Block #1
You Have Not Been Properly Educated

This one is very, very common. If you do not get enough information on what to look for, what to be aware of, and simply how Spirit Guides communicate with you, it is very hard to filter through all of the different avenues yourself. Even if you do a successful job, without verification, or the proper knowledge of signs to look for to help you verify you are on the right path, you will question yourself and brush it off. What I have noticed from years of teaching is that students who came to me were not getting enough information about how the whole communication process works. There are so many things that you need to be aware of, important things, and many of those were being left out. I am confident that I have covered all of those things here in this book. If I have left something out and you have a question that has not been covered, please go to my website and e-mail me; contact information will be at the end of the book. I will be happy to answer those questions for you.

Block #2
Your Belief System

Your belief system is something which you have spent many years working long and hard at creating; so do not be upset if you cannot seem to break down these barriers overnight. You have probably trained yourself for over ten years to not believe in spirits. Just think about it; every time you "feel" something behind you or get a block of thought from someone who has passed, you immediately brush it off as impossible. When people "feel" a presence, most of the time it scares the daylights out of them so they do whatever they can to not feel the presence anymore. Can anyone say "blocking"? There have been too many scary movies out there portraying the spirit world as evil or scary and something that can harm us (thanks movie industry). If you are not scared you tend to go another route: 'seeing is believing.'

People need to be able to "see" things in order to believe in them. If you cannot see something, like spirits, it is hard for you to wrap your mind around the possibility that they are real. To believe that spirits or Spirit Guides actually exist, is quite a magical feeling, because it is quite magical! What have you been told about anything that gives you that magical feel, like Santa Claus, the Tooth Fairy, or the Easter Bunny? Well, you see where I am going with this. It is more important, now than ever, to challenge and restructure your belief system.

Block #3
Your Sensitivity Level Is Low

This directly relates to Block #1 and Block #2, so this will change for you as you have gained the knowledge to raise your sensitivity by reading this book. Again, I know I am repeating myself, but you have spent many years trying not to "feel" spirits. So it is going to take some work to bring yourself "in tune" again. This tuning is a real thing. Imagine it like this: say you were a really good runner when you were young. Now that you are older, you have let yourself get out of shape and you do not run anywhere, you just sit at your desk all day. Then, you heard about a race you would like to attend. It is a couple of months out so you decided to enter. You would need to start taking the proper steps to tone your muscles again and get them prepared for the task ahead. You would need to work on your cardio so it could support your muscles and sustain your body during the duration of the race. Your muscles would not just go out there and perform to the best of their ability because you where asking them to. Just because you used to do it and you are fully capable of doing it. Without the proper training and exercises beforehand to help get you into shape, you would not perform very well. Spirit communication is the same thing, you are fully capable, but in order to do it properly there needs to be training and exercises in order to get yourself "tuned" up and back into shape.

Block #4
You Are Overlooking the Signs

Have you ever heard of the joke about the guy whose house was flooding? This man was at his house when a dam broke and water was coming towards his home, when a fire truck came by and told him, "You need to evacuate, your house is going to go under water."

The man was praying and said, "No thanks, God is going to save me."

The flooding was getting worse and the water had filled up the first floor of his house.

So the man went to the second floor and began praying when a boat came to his window and two police officers said, "You need to come with us, sir, your house is going to go under water soon."

The man turned to them and said, "No thank you, God is going to save me."

So they drove away in their boat to help other people. Then the water began rising to the second floor, so the man climbed onto the roof of the house and was praying, when he spotted a helicopter.

The rescue people yelled at the man through the loud speaker, "Sir, grab onto the ladder. You need to come with us or you are going to drown."

The man looked up and yelled, "No thank you, God is going to save me!"

So the helicopter left and the man drowned. When he got to heaven he was a little upset and said to God, "What happened? I thought you where going to save me?"

God looked at him confused and said, "I sent you a fire truck, a boat, and a helicopter. What more do you want from me?"

People do this often, overlook the obvious signs of help, or obvious answers to a problem they are having, because it is presented in a manner that seems too obvious. Do not limit your perception on the manner in which Spirit Guides will help and guide you. Many times people assume that the solution must be given to them in a complicated, woo woo, kind of way. This is not always the case, the solution might be right in front of you and your guides may have very well had something to do with it!

Block #5
Giving Up Too Soon

Like I mentioned before in Block #3, it takes some time to "tune" yourself in again and it will most likely not happen overnight. You need to be committed to learning how to communicate with your Spirit Guide for a period of at least six months. Don't try it for a couple of days or even weeks and then say, "It's not working!" If that's your plan, I will save you some time here and tell you now, you are right, it probably won't work. Your success depends on knowledge (gained here), practice (what you learned), challenging your beliefs (this part is actually fun and you should do this all the time anyway), being consistent, and being patient. Those things take some time, so do not give up too soon. I have taught thousands of people how to contact their Spirit Guides, and I have a huge success rate. All of this information has been gathered over more than twenty years of teaching and if you follow these things, I have no doubt in my mind that you too, will be successful!

Aloha! My name is Jennifer O'Neill and I am an Empath specialist...

I was born looking at the world differently than most everyone else around me. The funny thing is I thought everyone was like me.

It wasn't until I got older that I realized...I was born with a very special connection to the spirit world.

This connection has allowed me to access things you can benefit from. Lots of information on how things work in the spiritual realm, how things work energetically in the physical realm, as well as how this information can help you to enhance your life and help you to live the best life possible.

I was born a very strong Empath. I was gifted with this ability with a purpose, to teach others. To show you that you have some of these same abilities, and to simplify the process of using these spiritual tools and gifts you were born with in a way that fits into your everyday life.

Mahalo,

Jennifer

Jennifer is the author of several books and is also the creator and founder of Empath University. She is also one of Hawaii's top psychics and a leading expert in the field of spirit communication. She has spent the last twenty years as a professional psychic and spiritual teacher helping people all over the world learn how to develop themselves spiritually.

★ CONTINUE YOUR SPIRITUAL JOURNEY BELOW ★

Keys To The Spirit World >>>

www.keystothespiritworld.com >>>

★ FREE MEDITATIONS ★
(links at keystothespiritworld.com)

★ THE EMPOWERED EMPATH PODCAST★
(links at keystothespiritworld.com)

YouTube
Spotify
iTunes

★ EMPATH UNIVERSITY CLASSES ★
(link https://empath-university.com/)

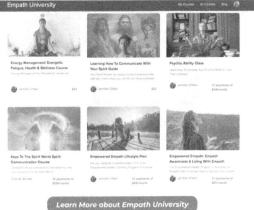

★ CONNECT WITH ME ★

instagram.com/keystothespiritworld

pinterest.com/keystothespirit

twitter.com/keystothespirit

Made in United States
Cleveland, OH
23 March 2025

15457714R00042